BRANCH IN HIS HAND

BRANCH
IN HIS HAND

Sharon Charde

The Backwaters Press

ALSO BY SHARON CHARDE

Bad Girl At The Altar Rail, Flume Press, 2005
Four Trees Down From Ponte Sisto, Dallas Community Poets Press, 2006

First printing November, 2008

The Backwaters Press
Greg Kosmicki, Rich Wyatt, Editors
3502 North 52nd Street
Omaha, Nebraska 68104-3506

thebackwaterspress@gmail.comt
http://www.thebackwaterspress.com

ISBN: 9781935218005

ACKNOWLEDGEMENTS

The author wishes to thank the editors of the publications where some of these poems first appeared.

JOURNALS

Caduceus: "His Death," "I Drag His Death After Me"
Calyx: "My Husband Loves Me"
Comstock Review: "Girl"
Homestead Review: "Four Trees Down From Ponte Sisto"
Illya's Honey: "Rome 1987"
Maryland Poetry Review: "For The Son Who Lives"
Poeticas: "Husband"
Voices In Italian America: "Long Marriage," "Cinque Terre," "Passeggiata,"
        "Wedding"
White Pelican Review: "At The Best Western"

ANTHOLOGIES

Proposing On The Brooklyn Bridge: "Anniversary"

PRIZES

"Choosing My Son's Cemetery Plot," Honorable Mention in Ed and Fay
        Phillips Prize, *Gulf Coast Magazine*
"For The Son Who Lives," Honorable Mention, Michael Egan Poetry
        Contest, *Maryland Poetry Review*
"Girl," Finalist in *Comstock Review*, Honorable Mention in Hill-Stead
        Museum's Sunken Garden Competition
"Rome, 1987," First Prize, Dallas Community Poets Competition
"Versions," Finalist, Dallas Community Poets Competition

CHAPBOOKS

Dallas Community Poets Chapbook Competition, First Prize: *Four Trees Down From Ponte Sisto*, "The Gift," Saying No," "His Death," "Four Trees Down From Ponte Sisto," "Pieta," "Grief," "Outliving Him," "Every Spring"

Flume Press Chapbook Competition, First Prize: *Bad Girl At The Altar Rail*: "Choosing My Son's Cemetery Plot," "I Drag His Death After Me," "Cinque Terre," "Wedding," "Passeggiata," "Termini Station," "Husband," "The Gift"

BRANCH IN HIS HAND

I

II

III

for Matthew, the son who lives

I

GIRL

just now I ate oatmeal with apples
the mowed field is under snow
a husband holds me in
his rough wool vest scratches my skin
I don't run but want to
feeling the thin young man
stirring inside him

she is gone, that girl
isn't she?
the one who sucked the sky
through a straw
who bled
who wanted God to love her

the bowl of my body empty now
blood stopped
baby dead
must I rewind her?

I try to think her under the snow
reduce her to a hard red stone
she brings me melons, pomegranates, prayers
she won't leave me alone

ANNIVERSARY

I was such a beautiful
bride, thirty-three
years ago, not yet
a wife. Look at me
in lace. I am happy,
promising anything.
He is smiling. We
have not yet become
coupled. The ground
springs under our feet,
we are facing the cave
but want to run
in the meadow
instead. Our life lies
ahead like our death,
we cannot see
it, we are in its footprints
and it will follow us whether
we want it to or not.

And here are the children,
the house and the dog,
the dirty sheets and towels,
casseroles and homework.
Here are the promises, made
and broken, and made again.
Here are the spokes of a wheel
spiked from a hub, turning,
the path made by taking,
the innocence made more innocent,
like a remedy for itself. Here
are the forests and the trees,
the locked rooms, the huddle over

death, yes, here are the bride
and groom holding their lifeless
child, waiting for the son who lives
to shine the ruin with his glistening
bride, to let the spelunking begin
again.

TRAIN RIDE NORTH

Manhattan. August. Piss
steams off the sidewalks.
Walking to Broadway we
plot dinner before the train.

The actors wear overalls, bright
jerseys. Runaways. Teenagers.
You are only twelve. I smell
you next to me, the theatre's
hushed mustiness.

Benihana's, we decide. You
love the drama of the high-
hatted chef. I'm sure I ordered
shrimp, you meat. He cooks
mine first. We begin to eat. Then
you turn to me and I reach
for the ventolin inhaler
in my purse, lay cash
on the table, pin my eyes
to your gray face and take
your hand. We are walking
through water, a force field
defied. It takes us a half-hour
to reach the sidewalk.

I will air from my lungs
into yours. *There now, we'll
cross the street. There now, we'll
enter the station.* I know I should
hail a cab, take you to a hospital,
but I don't.

If I can get you out you will
breathe. Your face chalk now
as I talk you through Grand Central,
walk down the dark ramp holding
your damp hand. I avoid your
eyes, find more pills in my purse,
press them on you. I pull you
up the steps to our seats, *Breathe,*
breathe, good air is coming. We're
in Westchester now. I open
the window. You're slumped
on the rough seat but I can see
the pink seep back
to your cheeks.

LUCE

A rosemary tree espaliered, Ricardo Bremmer's
white stucco studio on Via Castellaci. I didn't
see it until morning when the children playing
woke me, bouncing balls in bright Italian sun
calling to each other in language I don't understand.
I didn't know rosemary grew to trees with flowers,
purple cups, deep peach hearts. My son sleeps
across the courtyard. After months of separation
I move toward him.

To Cararra in an old white Peugeot, the day
a little misty. White marble mountains shrink us
to toy size, our car to a matchbox. Nothing
to do but look at those white cathedrals and think
of Michelangelo. My son wanders alone in the grandeur,
I chatter, nervous with awe. We all bend, choosing shards.
He finds the perfect shapes.

At da Roberto's, blue and white napkins, thick
golden wine, *melanzana,* carves and curls of pasta.
All of us around the table beginning to speak the new
language. I'm not remembering other marble, a child's
headstone in that walled square, *As you are I once was,
as I am so you will be.* My son running to me,
"Mommy, a little girl my age…died."

Venice closes after us, an island heavy with Easter.
The trains don't run. A Vivaldi *stagione* floating
in unnavigable air—we hum with it, walking. My son
waits at the bell tower but his friends don't come
for hours. *E Pasqua.* We climb cement stairs to the top
of da Gino. "My life is with my friends now," he says
and I cry. The island is sinking. We leave him,

take our weight to Rome. That night, my husband's dream—
our son lying in weeds by a river.

Reckless, he meets us in Rome, takes us to Cimitero
dei Cappuccini, altars of stacked sacra, a monk
with dirty hair, skull-crammed arches. He stands
near a pile of femurs, watching us. My husband
beckons me to a small sign ringed in wrist bones.
As you are I once was. As I am, so you will be.
At Termini Station we unload bags, our son's duffel
stuffed, purloined glasses wrapped in sweaters.
We'll carry it home.

This is what I notice: small, blood-colored stains
at the edges of dogwood petals, smell of azalea and
exhaust, everyone smoking and talking. He comes with us
to the airport bus, wrinkled blue striped shirt, bronze
leather jacket. I might have said *Ciao,* as I laughed
and kissed him, all of us shining in the space
of saying good-bye.

The parapet with him that day at Montalcino—
picnics, artichokes, *formaggio, vino russo, panne*
under olive trees near empty churches. Pasta
in the pale damask dining room at Via Altino, *trattorias,*
gelato, ruins, *antipasto,* and *caffè doppio.* All afternoon,
three of us roam the gold stone of my native land.
The light is Caravaggio's.

MAY 8, 1987

Fourteen years ago I sat on the deck in a purple bikini
replenishing my Amalfi Coast tan — later saw
a friend at the bank, told her what a wonderful
time we'd had with you in Rome. Oh, I was full
of stories—the Vivaldi concert we'd wandered into
off St. Mark's Square, the Vatican gift shop
with its Pope beer can openers and rosaries,
the Italian you and I had practiced each day
until I was good enough to go on my own
to the café down the street from your apartment
and ask for a *doppio, a pannini,* get change
and chat a little with the man behind the counter.
I hummed as I made the same tomato sauce
with mussels we'd had together at La Villeta
in Trastevere for dinner that last night.
The *News Hour* had an essay on Mother's
Day, I caught it going back to the deck
with our plates—oh, yes, Mother's Day
was Sunday, you'd still be in Rome. I'd miss you.

Your father, always up before me, answered
the phone the next morning. You were dying
while we slept. How could I not have known it?
The fire's burned down to ash by now but I still
see him, grey-faced in his blue and green bathrobe
with the chewed-up hem, holding the phone to his ear,
the black lab circling her empty dish, I see the last
sunny morning of my 45 years, I see you lying
by the Tiber, dead.

SAYING NO

Over the dreamhollow sound of the transatlantic cable that makes all voices into echoes. No, I screamed to my husband in a green and blue bathrobe with a rip on the left shoulder. Yes, he said. Yes. Here, you call. He walked very slowly away from the counter. I dialed the number, pushing the buttons down fast. A dark man's voice answered. *American Embassy.* My husband just talked to you, I said. From Connecticut. You told him a lie and I said I would call you for the truth. Please, the truth. *Madame, I am so sorry. Your son found at 8:10 this morning. In Trastevere, by the Ponte Sisto. Lying in the weeds.* No. You have made a terrible mistake. It is someone else's son. *Madame. He has been identified. American student. All his papers, student ID, in his wallet. His wallet in his pocket.* No. My voice was quieter. No. Not him, my baby, my boy, my man. You don't understand, I said to the man. He can't be dead. We just visited a week ago. He was to call this morning. *Madame, the Embassy regrets. All papers will be sent. Police will bring them.* No. No. No. Nothing more to say so I just repeat it like a mantra. I think I am not crying. I am writing "found by the Tiber" on a yellow legal pad. I still have the pad. No. I must have hung up. The man, my husband, on the other side of the room does not look like anyone I know. His face is grey, twisted. I do not yet know that I do not look like the woman who was sipping coffee ten minutes ago and will never look like her again. My hair is turning grey. Police come. No. Relatives are called. No. No. They all say it too. So many people and all I remember is the saying of No. Not you, not him, not here, not there. No. It gets quieter, but never sleeps.

ROME, 1987

The wisteria was especially purple
that spring, the dogwood dazzling
as we walked up the Aventine
to our son's school, his happiness
reaching out to us like another flower
drawing us forward full into its scent.
For nine months he had lived here
learning. How proud he was of his
Italian, that he looked like an Italian
in his leather jacket, he had become
Italian since he'd left us, my genes
had blossomed in him. He was fluent,
so filled with the language it had carried
us through Viarregio, Pietrasanta, Florence,
Venice, Siena, and Rome.

Though we were foreigners we were still
his kin, and he allowed our presence, this
Italian son. We left him to go home
wondering if he would ever want
to return. When the *carabinieri*
found him lying by the Tiber
that morning they even thought
he was Italian, an Italian drug addict,
they pushed up the sleeves
of his leather jacket looking for tracks.
What did they do with our boy then?
He already smelled of death, the night
had taken him. Did they put him
into an ambulance, take him
to a *pronto succorse*? No, that

would have been for saving a life—
it was our lives that needed saving then.

DREAM

The taxi flies by a Rome dripping
with summer, we huddle inside
clammy with the heat and sweat
and fumes, tourists of a new kind
now, not the ones of two weeks ago
buying *carciofi* and *formaggio*
pasta and *melanzana* at the big market
near his house for a dinner feast—
not the ones who clambered through
Cararra's marble caves stuffing
their pockets with shards—
not the ones who stood at St. Peter's
by the *Pieta* or waited in line
at the Uffizi, gelato dripping
down their chins.

You wanted to leave Venice,
practically pushed me onto the train—
Andiamo, andiamo you would have said
if the Italian words were at home
on your tongue. So we left him
to be there with his friends
and it was on the way to Rome
you told me the dream you'd had
the night before—*he was lying in weeds
by a river*—and so the seeds of death
were in our boy already. How relieved
we were when he came back that night
as if he'd been rescued from the river,
given back to us.

So we left him again in the Eternal City,
little wedge of worry tucked behind

our hearts, and when the Embassy called
ten days later, said he'd been found
by the Tiber, dead, we remembered
the dream. Why hadn't we told him
to be careful by rivers, to stay away
from weeds? Why hadn't we taken
that small opening from the other, more secret
world and offered it up to him?

HIS DEATH

because of waking up
we didn't sleep
three days and
over the ocean
concentrating
on one thing
maybe it wasn't true
but it was
and then at last
his apartment
16 Via Altina
near St. John Lateran
we told the driver
then the courtyard
then the elevator cage
his forks and dishes
tee shirts, notebooks
alarm clock
the new time
free fall into his
big blue quilt
two who made him
smelling him
we can sleep now
our bones lengthen
our teeth sharpen
our fingers clutch
the down

MOTHER'S DAY AT THE MORGUE

The room smells, phenol fumes,
tobacco smoke. The once-white
walls are grimed, but the sheets
that wrap him are pure as baby
swaddling. I know another mother
has bleached and ironed them for me.

He is under glass, a treasure.
Our hands grasp the hard angles.
I am crooning to my child, my hands
pressing their prints everywhere.
His eyes are closed. *He is sleeping
so peacefully.* The mothers at this place
of strange caring have washed
his hair, pulled it back from his forehead.
Soon he will wake and walk to me.

I am glad they have covered him.
I do not ask him to open his eyes.
My hands no longer feel glass but
his soft skin, the baby body I was
allowed to touch when he was mine.
I hear sounds in the room. Perhaps
they are coming from outside? Someone
is screaming *My baby, my child.* I try
to climb on the box. The men are kind,
they hold my hands. I want to hit them.

The room is hot and the doctors come
at us smoking their cigarettes like weapons.

I am holding the side of the box where
his hand is. My husband holds the other.
Why is our boy in a box?
A woman comes into the room. It is
my mother. *Why is her face so twisted?*
She has caught her daughter naked,
in the act of making love.

HAPPY MOTHER'S DAY

Spero, anche spero, the thin blue tissue is not
strong enough to hold these words. *Spero che
questo cartolina arriva in tempo.* I have just flown
over the Atlantic for the second time in two weeks.
Anche spero che hai un buon giorno della madre.
Sunday was Mother's Day, my son has sent a card
he fashions from Italian words, blue tissue airmailed
from the Vatican so it would arrive before he did.
Senza il tuo figlio. Io pensero di tui.

Your son who thinks of you. I sit on the white linen
of my living room couch, translating. The neighbors
have brought soft food, pasta, chicken, white wine.
Someone offers a plate, a glass. *Spero che questo
cartolina arriva in tempo.* I am wearing the same clothes
I've had on for four days. I clutch the blue tissue,
the block-lettered words. *Devi tradure questo cartolina
primo di io ritorno.*

Tomorrow is Thursday. The rosewood box sits
at Fioumicino, ready for loading as freight. *Con
amore, Geoff.* His boxed body dressed in tie-dyed
tee shirt, blue and white striped oxford. No shoes.
Dark green Air Force pants with lots of pockets.
We fastened a red bandanna around his neck before
we left. *Con amore, Geoff.*

The box, open, shaped more like a body than American
boxes. Women with scarves on their hair, muttering
rosaries , surround it. *So young, so young,* they
say in Italian. *Va t'en* I say to them as if they were gypsies
begging in Termini. Get away. I am *cara mama.* I want
them out. This is my son. *Salute! Con amore, Geoff.*

They want to offer support, prayers, this is the Italian way,
my son's teacher offers. *Tell them to go away. I don't want it.*
My words float among the red gladiolis, international flower
of the dead. I am wearing a dark green dress, black shoes
from Florence. *Io pensero di tui.*

I may have put some food in my mouth. It goes down
easy. I clench blue tissue, stare at the return address.
Figlio Charde, he has written. *Suore Camadolesi, Clivio
dei Publicii 2, Roma Italia.* It was near the Aventine, dogwood
full blooming. Our calves aching from the uphill walk.
A small man selling tissue boxes at the bottom. He wants
us to buy some. I pull Italian words from my mouth,
a twenty-thousand lire note from my pocket. *Figlio,
morte, wanted you to have this.* How my son had admired
this tissue-seller who stood with his goods in every weather.
I will give him twenty-thousand before I leave, he had said.
So I offer, insist. He wants me to take cartons of tissue.
I am going back to America and cannot take it. I notice
how thick the air is. He takes the lire, finally. *Grazie,
grazie, senora.*

We continue up the hill to Suore Camadolesi. I
have never seen dogwood so beautiful. *Cara mama.
cara mama, senza il tuo figlio.*

THE NIGHT OF THE DAY MY SON DIED

the night of the day
my son died
I spread the photos
of our last trip with him
all over the dining room table
desperate to find him
among the cafés and gardens
looking for him everywhere
among the churches and museums

I have to discover his smile
I am wild with wanting
to see it but mostly it seems
that he or someone else
has taken the photos
and there are only two of him
and he is not smiling

I forage in cabinets, closets, drawers
for more, family albums, loose
plastic bags of likenesses—
scatter them over couches and chairs
I'm as feverish as a gambler
pushing at the night
wanting to win
oh wanting to win

I'm crowding out grief with desire
that's why I have to find the picture
the one of him smiling
the one that will tell me
the dead can forgive

BEFORE THE FUNERAL

like a
bride

in my
black dress

they want me
to walk

down
the aisle

with you
in a box

I wash
my hair

sit wrapped
in a towel

someone
finds me

says I
have to

come
downstairs

the pumps
hurt my feet

the minister
wants hymns

he says
they make people

feel better
I say no hymns

my mother has
a bloody nose

outside
the church

an old friend
screams

David
wears

a tweed
jacket

with a plastic
pumpkin

in the
lapel

he pulls
a little string—

the pumpkin's
mouth

opens
and grins

in the vestibule
no gravity

they sit me
in a chair

prepare me
to do

what no
mother

should
ever

have
to

I MEET MATTHEW'S GIRLFRIEND AT HIS BROTHER'S FUNERAL

mom, I want
you
to meet her

eyes
make space
in the crowd

my pumps
stuck
in soft
May grass

honey-colored
she clings
to the edges

he worked
between

you were curled up in a ball wailing
she told me later

black dresses
salads from neighbors
picnic tables
under the oak tree

the green acre
of our yard
hundreds milling

a man went into the kitchen and asked for a gin

she didn't
know
where
the edge was exactly

too new
to be held by a group
too polite

morning after
their first full night together
I call (not knowing)

your brother's dead
right there mom

three hours later
police
documents
three of us
left

one week later
this

people pushing their way to me

terrible
terrible

I'm so sorry
sorry

my face
in mothball-smelling
men's chests

I think
I see her
flash of honey
on the edge

but I don't remember really

I want to lie down

mom please

CHOOSING MY SON'S CEMETERY PLOT

My boys were Catholic by the water
from Saint Francis de Sales on Baltimore,
West Philly. I stopped it by the time
they were three and four; it was the priests
preaching our badness that got to me.
I thought I'd teach them something else—
the meaning of life here, not hereafter,
how splendid dew looks on the tip of a leaf,
to hold a woman's hand in the light just before dark,
what comes after making love.
I don't know if I did.

When I called about the cemetery plot
Father wanted the baptismal certificate—
he must see it, the original. No burial
in sacred ground without one. After the seller
had checked our deed we were finally free
to inspect the subdivision of standing stones,
pick out a spot for his cement vault and us.
I was wearing Geoff's Grateful Dead tie-dye,
my husband and living son in shorts. *I like it here,*
No here is better, we'd call out to each other
in our macabre search. Torn, finally, between two
plots, we decided he'd be most at home
by the shed where they dumped the dead
gladiolas and browning Christmas wreaths,
near the open field.

MY HUSBAND LOVES ME

My husband loves me. He says
he does. He whispers it in the
dark, undercover like a strawberry.
The sheets are white with blue stripes.
They may be the same sheets we
slept on the night birds sang ten years ago.
I've not bought many new ones since.

Have you ever heard birds sing in the night?
I did, the day my son died. You see,
I could not sleep, sleep was impossible
of course, I must stress this. Closing
the eyes made movies; birthday parties,
the sheen of his hair, his red pants
at eighth-grade graduation, his round
glasses, brown bucks, backpack, his
little bear. How? Why? He's falling
screaming through the air.

My husband wanted to come in me, comfort
in his wife-house, he could not sleep either
and I said yes but my house is broken
and there was really no room and I had no
juice and I wanted nothing but my child
who I could not have.

In the rest of the rooms of my house
were a father, a mother, and maybe
two sisters. Or did they leave? I don't
remember. I don't know where they slept
or didn't, on couches, floors or beds. Or
if they heard the birds singing. In another
room, the son who lived. It was dark, early

spring. I could feel the heart being carved
from my ribs, the hair shafts shooting up
gray. My mind leaked all known language,
the purity of want filled the empty space, spread
tentacles to stripped skeleton.

My husband was heavy on me. No comfort
in our joining, only memory of making
the dead child. I was dry, juice drained
with the carving.

You don't get up when you haven't slept.
It just goes on, the phantom pumping,
the cells dividing, the kidneys cleaning
sugar out of blood. Friends put food
into an imagined mouth. They want
to keep you moving, Let's walk, they say.
They pray for grace, or time, or hiding.
They do not know you are not there.

Morning is only more moments of knowing.
He was found by the Tiber, dead. I stare
at hangers filled with clothes, reach
for some and pack for Rome. There are
planes and taxis. My husband loves me.
We will survive, he said. He's lost his hair.
I don't know why he loves me. I gave him
sons, no daughter. I've filled space with others.

And even though I've bought a new
mattress, the ghost of death is in our bed.

FOUR TREES DOWN FROM PONTE SISTO

there is no end to this
behind the mountains dense clouds
I come out to the sun
and it leaves

REPORT BY PROFESSOR ALVARDO MARCHIORI AND DOTT.
LUISA COSTAMAGNA ON THE DEATH OF

CHARDE GEOFFREY PATRICK

four trees down from Ponte Sisto
lying on his left side
branch in his hand

*on the morning of 5/9/87 the body of a youth later identified as Charde
Geoffrey Patrick, was found on the lower embankment of the Tiber near
Ponte Sisto*

it was late
wall of mossy
marble blocks
45 feet up
the sycamores

*the corpse...lay close to the edge of the wall of the Lungotevere (street that flanks
the Tiber). The body was taken to the city morgue at 1:40 pm on 5/9/87*

Madame, I'm afraid
some bad news
no not my son
Madame I'm afraid
it is

he was an American student who was in our city for study purposes

missed his exam
the call
the many calls
Alitalia Flight 1498
four seats
wherever you have them

a male 20 years of age, height 168 centimeters, weight 72 kg., cadaveric rigidity diffused but not too intense

did I say
he was lying
on his left side
it was late

he absented himself from his friends without ever returning

all these
people in our house
why
are they here

a small bloodstained area behind the left ear

we try
to put his earring in
too swollen

on the left side above the collarbone an abrasion...bones of the cranium were intact

did he scream

coming down

did he cry

Mom

Mom

Dad

Help

abdomen: walls intact; emperitoneo made up of about 1500 cc of blood, for the most part fluid, a black color

bled to death

in the night

alone

Mom

Dad

are you there

we testify the corpse was wearing the following clothes:

1) a leather jacket of brown color, which had a large tear in the area of the left sleeve (armpit) with the fragment of a leaf attached to it

2) pants of a jeans type of a light gray color with small leaves and branches attached to them

3) a white cotton shirt with thin gray and beige stripes, without collar

my child
here at last
you in a box
white sheets
wrap you
they've washed
your hair

namely,
it was a great trauma
caused by
a fall

DEATH IS HER SCULPTOR

death is her sculptor
fashioning new grooves in the aging
envelope of skin and flesh
and feeling
finding the bones
carving his shape into them
he chisels hard
stopping
for no rest these days
of suffocating summer
it's not a neat
process
this dark work
and there is dust
sifting from her
blank white
marble stare

FOR THE SON WHO LIVES

I watch you like a movie rolling towards its close,
sure I know the ending, sure I don't.
On a Saturday morning in May it started, this watching.
My eyes began to decorate your every move,
fix on that narrow body so like your father's young one,
so different from the soft dead brother's.
Now, unashamed, I feast fully on your arms, your legs,
the way your chin juts out, the voice that moves
from your mouth into the air around you. I make prayer
from your slender hips and the nose that looks like mine,
celebrate the way you walk and cock your head in careful listening.
I notice your neck and the way your hair has darkened,
that you still breathe through your mouth in sleep.
When I laugh at your jokes I do it double time,
make you twice alive. I am so grateful
for the timbre of your voice, the photos of you yesterday,
the brown boxes of Tin Tin books you keep forgetting
to retrieve from the closets of our home that is still your home.
I'll get them, Mom, you say and I hear *Mom* and sing
with you the word though you don't know it.
You made me a mother. He came and went in the middle,
your brother. You make me mother still. I want more of you,
double, triple, children from your flesh, insurance
that your body will be here when mine is not,
promises of old age for us both,
I want you to tell me you will fall off no walls,
never be in the path of an oncoming car,
keep your organs exercised, well-fed,
let no cells that don't belong in you begin.
That's right, I want to keep you from harm forever,
wrap you in cotton, know where you are.
After all, I'm your mother, it doesn't stop, this state of grace
we inhabit together. But just in case, I watch.

BUILDING A HOUSE

The old barn gapes at us
from tall grass
with its window-eyes.
Open doors list
in the island wind.
So forlorn! Surrounded
by its smaller siblings—
outhouse, toolshed, red
shack growing vines, even
an empty foundation
of teetering boulders.

We park our bikes,
climb the ladder
to the loft, see the square
of sky and sea—
the ocean's blue heart
beating in our barn.

Somehow with the ocean
keening on four sides
I am willing to be shattered.
Necessary signing of papers.
Not a whole piece in me.
Only the echo of breaking.

Shipments of shingles, friends
to hammer them on after
the gutting. Use of the saw,

blue lines snapped smartly,
nails from my apron. Water
and wind wail always
outside. Roof beams coming
by boat, sections of floor.
Big bales of insulation, two
truckloads packed with pink.
Thick glass panes in wooden
muntins nesting easy into sawed-
out space.

Laboring steadily we slice
two-by-fours for trim. Hunks
of sheetrock make our walls.
The white harrier hawk swoops
circles around the place; butterflies
tilt and whirl. In the seethe of the sea
I sleep, but somehow there are doors
hinged to openings, latches
fastened shut.

The sea's borrowed heart begins
to beat in me.

THE OLD WOMAN AND THE SEA

I.

This woman is waiting for the kindness
of stone and water, the grain of her skin opens
to receive it, pores scramble to seize
the first information of salt, of cold smooth
rounds of solid earth to place beneath her feet.
We can see so little of her, just a damp curl
of grey hair, loose clothing that could be
anybody's. She seems almost at home in stone,
water at her back, but too alone to make that fact.
Here, look her in the face carefully, see
how something has eroded her, we can only
wonder what. She sits on the ocean's skirt
like any other thing that is found there,
fissured by weather, cracking open with need
to receive the grace of a clear day.

Down the beach a bit gulls gather, grab
at shreds of dead fish, wait, flapping, for more.
They know the fluctuations of feeding. We
want to give this woman something to get her
standing, moving out of this picture toward
a kinder landscape, maybe a summer garden.
But she is fixed into this vista like the spray
and craze of water, she stays, holding
her bouquet of stones.

II

Stay away from me. I belong
to the sea, to stones that comfort,
rose quartz veined in white,
striped grey, plain ochre, even green.
I am wrapped in rock. Get back.
There is nothing but riptide here.
I won't look up if you come close.
I have cliffs you can't see,
high tide coming, sun stinging.
It's all here in damp sand, dump of ocean rock.
I've all the flesh and bone I need.
Gulls, crabs will teach the way to excavate a clam,
drop it just so to crack the shell,
expose the meat. I'll eat with them.
You won't see. Go home,
please.

III.

What is it you see, wrapping
your lens around the black-and-white
woman on the black-and-white beach?
Shoot her, your friend's mother not smiling,
the true woman in a moment of unshown
tearing. Did you want to dig this
from her daily smiles, set this photo against
the dinners of fish and wine, wedges of good bread,
did you want to mine this anguish from
the chatter in the back of the pickup, that walk
on the fog-soaked jetty? Everyone has an undertow.
But you're too young to see this in me, this sad
woman who lets you. Dressed in her sea and stone
clothes she just sits there without placards.
You caught her in an off moment. Take her, girl,
and know that she is at least part of what you
will grow into.

IV.

I've got to shine her some, she is
so unsung. I want to make her show up,
not seem unseen by the sea, another
piece of scrabble on its side. I know
how fine she is, how she draws smiles
over sadness, opens strong arms to take me in.
I want you to know this, and that she is a woman
whose son fell through the air a night in Rome
six years ago. Anyone could have fallen.
He lay there on stone in the dense May
dark, alone. How does she stand it?
You see all that sorrow in my photo, there's
too much of it, I think. I'll take another
so you can see how fine, how strong she is.

THE OLD WOMAN LEAVES THE SEA

I cut my hair, threw it at the desert sage.
My curl is natural; this picture is a cage.
I'm leaving it. I've had my time among
stones and water. I'm going to the garden.
I want black earth, bronze mud, yellow
daffodil, green grass. I want to ride a bicycle,
sing *a cappella*. I want to take the train to Rome.
I've put all my eggs in one basket. I'll get clothes
that fit. I've finished fasting. I'm definite.

I lie back to stare at the sky. It's another day
in the life of my grief. There's water everywhere.
I'm not doing enough, just gathering stones,
sitting here by the sea. I'm not the only mother
whose son has died. Why do I think I deserve
to laze here after seven years? I move my leg
right, then left, against the sand, watch
for an opening between sky, water.

FLIGHT 1280,
DALLAS/FORT WORTH

High in the cloud desert I wonder
if you swim in these cumuli,
if I could break this window with my small fist,
fly through a jagged hole I'd make,
sit us on silver plane-wing,
talk in some language of the last seven years,
ask how you have gone beyond boy.

Can you breathe without wheezing?
I'd want to know. *Are you getting enough to eat,
do you have friends?* I'd ask, feeling the cloud-wet
damp my hair to curl. You'd wonder
how I'd gotten gray,
if your brother was telling us jokes,
your father as silent.

Your dying did it, I'd say about the hair,
and *yes, he makes us laugh like you did,*
and *your father talks to flowers now.*

TUESDAY NIGHT YOGA

I send my brave living
mudras
asanas
a breath of fire
exhaled
to your box across the street
among
the standing
stones

COME WITH ME

for a long time
there were signs—

the note that said *It's a gift*
signed with his name *Geoff*
from the man who'd cut up our wounded oak for nothing

the new license plate on the Subaru
all the letters and numbers
adding up to the day he was born

and the dreams!

him at ten, almost always
except for the one when he lectured me:

don't blame anyone or anything for my death

everything but the signs and dreams
seemed strange to me
in this world without him

I wasn't ready
to be finished with death

I wasn't ready
not to find him everywhere

so I made myself into several women:

the one who shuffled
the raw wild cards of loss

the one who was terrified
to live with mercy and forgiveness

the one who lived only
to take care of the dead child

SEPARATING

everything
where it was
last summer
white table
two couches
red rug on polished pine

carrying in provisions
I stop to look
at the sea from the window
still blue

but things are dying
outside
or already dead

I put cheese and milk away
beans and rice
in the cupboard
clothes
on bedroom shelves
my toothbrush
by the sink

how careful
I am
as if
the position of things
mattered to someone

I take the days
whole
a parade
of foolishness

pretending
I am not a wife
or mother
harder than I
thought possible

snow comes
to the island
I love
the blue of the sea
against that white
but my hunger
never leaves me
instead it grows
monstrous

each day we bargain
my huge hunger and I

I think sleeping alone
will cure me
one place at the table
make me holy
that God will come
to this lonely
wind-slammed island
with His thunderbolt
of grace

just because
I need it

LONG MARRIAGE

I tried leaving you once, moved
to our summer place. The wind screamed
at me, *Go home, go home, don't stay,* but I
couldn't. Was that the winter you bought
me the sanctuary bell from Arcosanti?
I didn't let you come until Easter, you
would have brought it then, a brass nun
hitting a gong, to hang on our house.
It was poorly positioned to catch the wind
and gouged the house instead. I made
you the same salmon with red peppers
and artichokes I'd made for my lover. You
liked it, asked if you could stay the weekend.

We slept in the big log bed, a double white
line down the middle, but I could smell you.

Even though the garden was not yet aroused
from winter, you went to it the next morning—
maybe planning tomato plants, or where
to put new dahlias, as if we would be starting
the spring together. Something had loosened
between us, we felt it as we rode our bikes
to the beach, sat and drank coffee on the sand
of the island we'd come to after our boy
had died. I felt fuller somehow, more
corpulent, as if a thing I'd lost had been
reattached. But when it was time for you
to board the ferry, I had not said I was
coming back. You had not asked.

IV

VITA NUOVA

I.

Nothing fits. I'm disappearing.
Even my lips are thin.
I'm learning from them how to kiss
a man again. In Italy last year I was
apprenticing. I filled these clothes
out then, a mother still full of her
dead son.

II.

We walk to the wall you fell from, four
trees down from Ponte Sisto. My heart
is cold against the stone. Everyone else
is sweating. My husband takes my hand.
The grass is ten years higher, the sycamores
are taller. We climb down to the Tiber,
one white flower blooming where you
landed. I arrange roses in a boy's shape.

III.

We climb hills in our green car, pass
rows of drooping sunflowers, drink
vino russo and flirt at café tables.
Sebastian is everywhere shot with
arrows. In Spoleto I eat three plums.

Our car runs over a cat on the way home
from Montalcino. I begin to pray.
By day we are scattered across gold
fields, at night gathered in a shuttered
room.

IV.

England, green and sheep, birds
in hedgerows. I'm here to breathe,
my room a single bed and chest.
The nuns have left their convent
to the birds and us, my memories
of you. The walls are stone.
Nothing happens. The days go by.
I hike the lanes to Denbury, listen
to the sheep bleat. I dream
I am a girl in a burn unit,
wrapped in plastic.

V.

We leave the brick ghost where you
still live for a red house two-hundred
years old. We come quietly, breathing
in its dust and webs. My naked feet
touch old boards, my bare hands his
soft thigh skin. The kitchen is a white
square of sun. He carries me over
the threshold, we picnic and kiss.
All bones now, I whisper
your name.

VERSIONS

forty-five feet from the top
of a wall

the absence of music

San Giorgio in Velabro
cheap purple ribbon on flowers
his name in gold letters
a priest who spoke English

pick anything you want
to believe and believe it

Suore Lucia on her knees
in the garden   Suore Lucia
in her habit   holding me
we smile for the picture
my husband takes

how do you stand it

I am the mother

heavy clusters
of unripened kiwis
hang from arbors
like bouquets
of stones   leaves
make patterns on the sun

pick anything you want
to believe and believe it

he fell and my life

Suore Lucia has keys
that open all the doors
she takes us to the room
of the recluse   alone here
for forty years   a wooden
box   raised crucifix her bed

she wanted to die on that bed
but I moved her to a chair

the convent walls thicken,
we cool in the heat
Suore Lucia opens one door
after another   belt of thorns
cross of nails   other scourges

I couldn't stand her suffering

I'm the mother and I can't do anything

when you wake, I will comfort you.

forty-five feet
a flag from Siena over
his coffin   lilacs

pick anything and believe

Tom says *I watched a show about suicides, how they take off their shoes first. I*
didn't want to tell you.

shoes and glasses on the wall
branch in his hand

how do you stand it
I pick something to believe

autopsy: *the most reliable hypothesis is that of an accidental death*
branch in his hand

ROME, 1999

Report of death:
American citizen abroad

we have to
walk to the next set
of stairs, ours blocked
(they're rebuilding *Ponte Sisto*)
single file
through the weeds
syringes and used
condoms
sucking mud

Place of death: Tiber river bank,
Trastevere

my black
shoes on uneven
cobbles a thousand
years old, walking away
from my business
at the wall
out our window
the coliseum, gladiators

Disposition of the remains:
shipped

we carry yellow freesia
to the nun's garden
a fissure in the wall like
a wound, I run
my finger over

it rains every day
the shower leaks

Cause of death: ruptured spleen
internal bleeding

mothers and dead sons in
every museum
he died for our sins
my feet burn
in the Vatican

Passport #6580804 cancelled
and returned

HUSBAND

tonight I heard tree frogs singing
saw a field so luminous and green it was the ocean
I have come back
though there are still some shadows
under the deathbed
we have risen from

TERMINI STATION 2001

You asked me once,
when would I have divorced you?

On a swirl of chocolate-colored cobbles
outside Termini, I considered. We'd said good-bye
to him here all those years ago—you'd gotten me
away from the tracks to revisit this place,
remember it. I noted a *tavolo caldo*, a *caffe*,
an *alimentaria*, a rent-a-car. Good-bye,
arrevedervci, right here by the *autoleggio*, another
pizzeria, The Hotel *Siracusa*. Good-bye, *ciao*,
at Termini, his feet on this stone, the smells of Rome
around us—we stand today touching where those feet
had touched. The city has a burning smell, smoky still
though it's September.

Perhaps in Philadelphia, when the boys were young
and I hid my head under the table screaming, perhaps
in the hollow echo of my first faithlessness,
perhaps before moving to Connecticut. But how
could I leave you after we held our dead boy
in that dark room, after you tried to unwrap
his starched white swaddling, after we waited
together in the morgue for them to pull him
from his numbered steel slab?

There was no way to call for help. Before we
married I was loose sky, you bound me in. I
knew how not to be loved yet you loved me,
I remembered that as we flew home alone together.
I know you won't ask me again.

WEDDING

We're in Cortona and you wake on the third night
screaming, slicing the late September air with your
cries. Chiesa di Santa Domenico—I kneel
by a gold-leaf virgin with seven swords in her heart,
light a candle. All around are bunches of dying
white flowers. I think there must have been
a wedding here, yes, it's Sunday. The bride
and her consort walked through these cypress trees,
up this cobbled path to the pierced Mother of God
and spoke their vows. Were they comforted
by her pain as they entered their life together?
I am, here in my hiking boots and shorts,
so far from betrothal. All over Italy are dead
sons held by their mothers—marble, plaster,
gesso, triptyched, mine—no fathers.

Look, I say to you, *look at this carved-up woman
with all these swords in her heart.* Her calm expression
belies anguish, however, and perhaps that is what you see
as you glance over. The fourteenth-century church
is cool while heat shrieks outside. You don't
remember screaming.

DISORDER OF DESIRE

I cannot cure myself of desire
for things to be other
than how they are.
Take the Catacombs—
we'd been in Rome so many times
but never there. He'd been
though, and I wanted to go.
Christians had buried their dead
in this clandestine place
outside the city, but the emperor must
have known. Did they cart off the chewed-up
bodies from the Coliseum ring,
go by night to dig the *tufa* graves
in the malleable earth this site was famous for?
What did they use for light?

Well, we were both still above ground.
I wanted to walk right into those ruined
tombs, lay my body in one of the niches
carved out for martyrs here under the city
my son had died in. I wanted to sit
a fourth-century deathwatch
with the other ghosts. The guides spoke
at least five languages. We went
with the English-speaking. He
wouldn't let me lie down
and only took us to a small section
of the maze. You walked a little
behind me, with the Australians.
I wanted to stay, keen with the echoes,
be funereal, enter all this bereavement,

but you were already at the exit counter
buying souvenirs of the ruins. Defeated,
I joined you.

CINQUE TERRE

I lie naked on the bed at the Nazionale—
outside my window I see tiled roofs stretching
to the mountains we crossed today. You get up
to pull curtains across.

When we make love I see the evil in my soul,
imagine it like the liver spots near my ear
and on my cheek, distinct from the clearer
skin—all the sins gathered from my bad
girl's past, fulminating. You don't seem to
notice, speak of the quality of *vino russo*
at dinner, the *tartuffo* at lunch, stroking
my nipple.

Ecco-la! my soul shouts, look at these ashes.
This morning I lit a candle in Chiesa di San Pietro.
We hiked all day, feet on tops of old stone
walls, hairline paths through vineyards, smooth
basalt in cypress groves, the sea always shining
somewhere. We got higher and higher above it,
stopped for *colazione* in a circle of olive trees. Near
us, another man and woman, feet dangling
dangerously over the edge of a cliff.

Va bene. What is it I need to promise?
You fall asleep holding my arm.

PASSEGGIATA

Americans in Rome are being cautioned.
Rome, Italy perhaps a focus for terrorist acts in October.
—*International Herald Tribune*, October 2, 2002

Portovenere to La Spezia by boat,
the train to Pisa, eating olives, eggplant
soaked in oil, *foccacia.* Firenze, our hotel
an old *palazzo* with frescoes on the ceiling,
mirrored armoire—our voices echo
in the huge room. You've bought me
black lace underwear from a shop
on the Via del Corso. I pose in it
on the big bed laughing.

I think I will be mended here. Gangs
of motorbikes speed like shots under
our window—fumes, sirens, car alarms—
people laughing. In the Brancacci Chapel
we see Adam and Eve, later picnic
on a sunny curb by the Uffuzi. I toss crumbs
to a pigeon with a club foot and read
the *Tribune.*

The impossible *duomo* arises from nothing,
taking over the city. You want to wander.
I want the map, want to tick off memories
of our last times here. It's something to do.
Fifteen years ago I was locked in a bathroom
at Acqua al Due while you ate pasta with our son
and his friends. No one missed me. He and I
at the jazz concert on this corner, and there,
under the bridge, where we bought him
the leather backpack he wanted so.

Somewhere in Rome the terrorists plan
their attacks while we walk these gritty streets,
a tribe of two.

FIRST-AID KIT

It was the last day, after you'd taken
the #95 bus to Via Veneto and changed
our tickets. We set off for Ostia Antica.
Francesco said the port city's ruins had been buried
so deep in the Tiber mud that they were perfectly
preserved, and we should make the pilgrimage.
It was hot, maybe 90, as we walked down
Marmorata to the Pyramid and caught
the train to the west of Rome. He'd said
it would take about a half hour.

I felt delicate, like I had a long crack
up my side. Restless, sweaty, I waited
for the stop. We began walking where
the signs led but there were no crowds.
A woman coming over the bridge told us
Chiuso, Lunedi. I refused to believe her
though everything pointed to her being
right. The ruins were closed.

According to the map there was a beach
two stops away. I moaned I had no suit,
wanted to go back to Rome. Remember
how cheerful you were? Though naturally
you would be, you always are when I find no exits.

In the end, we went to the beach. It was your fault,
of course, that the ruins were *chiuso* and that
I had no towel. Sullen, I walked ahead of you
to the dark Italian sand. All the houses
were shuttered, after all it was mid-October.

When our dead son was ten, he'd wanted
a first-aid kit for Christmas—imagine! I didn't
know you'd put it in your backpack again,
pulled it out now, one of its tools a tiny
rectangle of folded foil, opened like origami
for our beach blanket. I stripped off my clothes,
ran into the cool sea. You went to find our lunch—
gamberini on *rugula, pannini,* tiny glasses of white wine,
big ones of *aqua minerale.* What else was in that kit?

Repair patches, the gauze bandage you'd put on my arm
when I fell on the path to Manorola, matches.

RITUAL

They're sitting in Trilussa Plaza—Ponte Sisto's
across the street, repaired since the last trip.
It seems the whole area has had a recovery;
the riverside is tidy, and large basalt squares
have been laid on the place he fell to. A dog
and two men are sitting in the exact location
of their son's dying, and so they wait before
going down. He suggests they throw the flowers
into the Tiber this time, but she says no, fears
the *carabinieri* might arrest them for littering.
And he didn't die in the river, she says
for emphasis.

They have stopped at a *fiorista;* she holds the cone
of six white roses, baby's breath. In a few days
they will go home, but today they walk slowly
down the stairs to the place under the fourth tree
from the bridge. The men have left. The sycamores
along the wall glimmer in the early evening light.
Solemn, they perform the ceremony, lay the flowers
down in the shape of him at twenty—one from his brother,
one from his brother's wife, one for each of their two boys,
themselves. She is careful to place hers where the heart
would be.

Then, a photo of her in black against the wall. They're
starting to think about dinner, shall they go to da Lucia?
It's not a long walk.

They take hands, rise up the stairs gladly, refugees
once more from all the summers and springs, the winters
and falls, from the sycamores, the bridge, the wall.

V

AT THE BEST WESTERN

Across the small shining pool I see a boy
about ten, narrow body, loose nylon suit,
and then there you are rising out of him
like steam, in your own ten-year-old body,
navy trunks with the two red stripes down the side,
wet hair sticking to your forehead, you've just
gotten out of the pool and are calling me
to come and look at something on the other side.
Your bathing suit is drenched and droopy but you
are widely smiling, you've always loved
the water, want me to come in with you now,
swim the length of the shimmering rectangle.
Slowly I rise to move toward you, dive in
and then of course you are gone but the water
takes me in and I begin to stroke, first the crawl,
then I'm on my back and then over on my breast,
laps and laps, my legs kicking then scissoring, heart
deep in the chlorinated liquid, not drowning.

COME BACK

for Geoffrey

I thought you would come back
as something, your brother's baby
or the rosebush Andrea gave me
for my birthday—the white hawk
that circled our backyard, the lab puppy
we got two years after you died.

I don't know which you were—
the rosebush shriveled and the hawk
doesn't come any more. The baby
is too much like his father. The puppy,
maybe, though he's grown into a sweet
old beast who surely will die within the year.

Does that mean you're twice gone?

Some days, I know I can hear you.
In Greece last month, Aghios Sophia—
the stack of bones in the sarcophagus—
(Dad says that's what you are now)
and then there was the purple cyclamen
blooming so improbably on the rocky path—
the red and white boat just like yours
beached in Stavri.

Mom, they all said, *listen to me.*
I've led you this far, keep going.
I say to the bones and the flowers,
I want you to know something
about your mother now—

having undone the padlock of your death
she has quieted.

But I want to see you in your tee shirt
and jeans, the red bandanna tied
around your brown hair, I want
to hear you whistle, tell me jokes—
to see you walk across a room
towards me smiling. I want you
to come back as yourself, not as
a boat, a bird, or a pile of bones.

PIETA

blood blossoms
on the cheap rayon lining
of the leather jacket
he bought in Florence
all around him
the Tiber's birthings
empty syringes
broken wine bottles
sticky condoms
skin of a dead rat

there are echoes
beneath the Ponte Sisto
a wall looms near

was the moon interested?
did anyone see him fall?
did he call out *Mom, Dad*
into the hot Roman night?

he will be replaced
by information
memory
imagination

he will be replaced
by a straw bag of letters and cards
a blue file folder in an oak drawer

he will be replaced
by therapists
broken vows
too many glasses of wine

he will be replaced
by trains and planes
a Land Rover bumping over a narrow road
on the Osa peninsula in Costa Rica
grilled sardines in Portugal
Rigoletto performed outside in Prague

he will be replaced
by a granite gravestone
two new houses
a black dog
his brother's marriage

he will be replaced
by 500 American soldiers
killed in Operation Iraqi Freedom
a barn full of dry wood burning
his grandmother's new heart

he will be replaced
by a squirrel's nest
made of black plastic and twigs
high on the farthest branch
of a just-blooming tree

my son is bleeding to death

he   will   be   replaced

FENWAY PARK

for Matthew

you told me it was complicated
that I would have to take a lot of trains
you told me I wouldn't like the food
but you, alone!
wearing a red shirt I had given you
brown lace-up shoes
a man's shoes
you told me it might get cool
I brought a jacket
we were in the wrong seats
had to move
so many umpires in this game
fast hard pitches
you explained all the rules
the night was red and getting redder
so glad I left him home
the dead one, your brother

in the top of the eighth our team made nine runs!
we cheered and cheered
I even drank a beer
our team won
sitting close to you on the hard seats
my son, my living son

DAY OF THE DEAD

I go to your grave for comfort—
letters cut into stone
your name
your birthday
your death day
triangle of granite
rocky offerings
at its foot
always the same.

I rip out the chrysanthemums
your brother and I planted in August,
fill the hole with soil dug
from behind our barn.
I've brought a small pumpkin,
some bittersweet— it's Halloween.
Our dog roams the other stones
while I sit on your bones
having my conversation with air.

GRIEF

an absolute purity
within the borders
and without
cacophony

everything slow
like the shimmer of heat
off summer asphalt

everything dry
like grains of dirt
in a drought

a hummingbird whirring
at the honeysuckle
hollyhocks higher
than the barn roof

all equal here
a shared condition

doesn't everyone die?
doesn't everyone seek rapture?

and this is rapture, really
the untainted longing
the total clarity
the utter, immaculate emptiness

I DRAG HIS DEATH AFTER ME

I drag his death after me, its details
a kind of communion, taking him in
day after day, him becoming my body,
my blood, I becoming his, we are
co-mingled in a way that would not
be allowed if he were alive. I remember
the phone call from the embassy, my *No,*
your face, the airport, our questions,
the one red gladiola smashed in the center
of the courtyard at the morgue. I remember
us alone in the dark room, him out of the box,
wrapped in starched white swaddling that your
hand reached to uncover, then stopped. We
stood over our boy like Mary and Joseph
in the manger, as if he were a new baby
blessedly fresh to the world. But it was his
death that was new, that we crooned to,
his death a presence in the room like some
terrible gift, that would be opened again
and again, that never stopped giving, only
we didn't know that then, we didn't know
how we would bring it home, where we
would put it, how we would live with this
present, how we continue to.

CONTRITION

for Matthew

I beatified your brother
took up all the space
that belonged to you
with my distress

I couldn't even smell you

each day I burned incense to his memory
stroked my death necklace of bones and breath

your brother
your brother

god-ghost in our family
not the living son

not his friends
his wife
his three boys

my mind chanted
my loss
my loss

my heart tangled around
his body in the box

long ago you decided to live
long ago you decided to forgive

OUTLIVING HIM

for Geoff

Your ghost blooms with the lilacs—
nothing takes away May's missing you,
not the bluebirds your father's enticed
at last to our backyard,
not the ravenous red tulips
or the luminous acres of lawn.
You bring death to the newly born.

It's not that I forget you in winter,
but winter's flowers are underground,
sheltered by hard earth—
not the outrageous bursts of spring
I cannot hide from.

Your death day sounds its arrival
with dogwood and daffodils
while your mother, now grey-haired and lined,
survives at winter's edge
unwilling still to outlive you.

EVERY SPRING

every spring
my dead son
whistles "Rockin' Robin"
in the Palio
in Siena with us

every spring
my dead son
stuffs his pockets
with marble shards
in Cararra's caves

every spring
my dead son
doesn't graduate
from college

every spring
my dead son
lies down
on the wall
in Trastevere
and doesn't know
what happens next

THE GIFT

my baby was dying
as it was being born

I didn't listen when death was talking to me
he stalked the flowers in my garden
filled the ground with seed
murmured at the celebrations

not yet   not yet

he brought me two baskets

in one, he said, put what is already dying
in the other, what is not yet dead

but they're both the same, I said

now I use one basket for what I don't know
and the other, for all I have lost

APPENDIX

MOTHER'S DAY CARD

Cara Mama,

Spero che questo cartolina arrive in tempo. Anche spero
hai buon giorno della madre—senza il tuo figlio. Io pensero di tui.
(Devi tradure questa cartolina prima di io ritorno!)
Salute!

Con Amore,

Geoff

Dear Mom,

I hope this card arrives in time. And I hope you have a happy
Mother's Day—without your son, who thinks of you. (I hope
this card arrives before I do!)
To your health!

With love,

Geoff

ABOUT THE POET

Sharon Charde, a retired family therapist, has been leading workshops and weekend retreats for women in Lakeville, Connecticut and Block Island, Rhode Island, since 1990. Since 1999 she has taught a weekly creative writing workshop with juvenile offenders at Touchstone, a residential treatment facility in Litchfield, as well as a monthly workshop with the Touchstone girls and students at the Hotchkiss School in Lakeville since 2002. In June of 2004 she edited and published a full-length anthology of their poetry, *I Am Not A Juvenile Delinquent,* which won the 2005 Literature PASS Award (Prevention for a Safer Society) given by the National Council on Crime and Delinquency in California.

Sharon has studied with Natalie Goldberg, Sharon Olds, Brenda Hillman, and Marie Howe. She has been published in *Caduceus, Calyx, The Comstock Review, Crosscurrents, The Homestead Review, Illya's Honey, The Maryland Poetry Review, Ping Pong, Poeticas, The White Pelican Review, The Women's Studies Quarterly,* and *Voices In Italian America;* in an anthology on marriage, *Proposing on the Brooklyn Bridge;* and a mother-baby anthology, *Not What I Expected.* She has received Honorable Mentions in contests sponsored by The Maryland Poetry Review, *Gulf Stream Magazine* and The Connecticut Poetry Society, and was chosen finalist in the 2001 and 2004 Comstock Review Contest, and the 2003 Hill-Stead Museum's Sunken Garden Poetry Contest, and won third prize in the 2003 Connecticut River Review competition. Her full-length collection, *Branch In His Hand,* won Honorable Mention in the 2005 Bordighera Bilingual Poetry Book Publication Competition. Flume Press, California State University, published her first prize-winning chapbook, *Bad Girl At The Altar Rail,* in September 2005. Six of her poems have been nominated for the Pushcart Prize. In 2006 her second prize-winning chapbook, *Four Trees Down From Ponte Sisto,* was published by Dallas Community Poets Press.

In the fall of 2005, Sharon was presented with the first Inge Morath Award given by The Trinity Arts Series, the University of Connecticut Torrington Campus, The Litchfield County Writer's Project and Zeeland Productions, for her creativity and the significant impact she has had on social development in the arts. On April 10, 2007, she was presented with the Making a Difference For Women Award given by the Soroptimist International of Connecticut, a worldwide organization for women in management and professions, working through service projects to advance human rights and the status of women, for her work with the young women of Touchstone.

She is mother to two sons, grandmother to three boys, and has lived in Lakeville, Connecticut, since 1970 with her husband, John.

Printed in the United States
139122LV00001B/28/P